I0190355

A COLORING BOOK
THE TEN COMMANDMENTS

LORRIE HARDIN

לֹא תִרְצַח	אָנֹכִי ה
לֹא תִנְאָף	לֹא יִהְיֶה
לֹא תִגְנֹב	לֹא תִשָּׂא
לֹא תַעֲנֶה	זָכוֹר אֶת
לֹא תַחְמֹד	כַּבֵּד אֶת

God gave the ten commandments to Moses.

I
II
III
IV
V

VI
VII
VIII
IX
V

EXODUS 19:20

AND THE LORD
CAME DOWN UPON MOUNT SINAI, ON THE
TOP OF THE MOUNT: AND THE LORD
CALLED MOSES UP TO THE TOP OF THE
MOUNT; AND MOSES WENT UP.

EXODUS 20: 2

I AM THE LORD THY GOD, WHICH HAVE BROUGHT THEE OUT OF THE LAND OF EGYPT, OUT OF THE HOUSE OF BONDAGE.

I

You shall have no other God's before me.

YOU SHALL HAVE NO OTHER GOD'S BEFORE ME.

II

Thou shalt not make unto thee any graven images.

THOU SHALT NOT MAKE UNTO THEE ANY GRAVEN IMAGES.

III

Thou shalt not take the name of the Lord thy God in vain.

THOU SHALT NOT TAKE THE NAME OF THE LORD THY GOD IN VAIN.

IV

Remember the Sabbath day and keep it Holy.

REMEMBER THE SABBATH DAY AND KEEP IT HOLY.

V

Honor your father and mother.

HONOR  YOUR FATHER AND MOTHER.

VI

Thou shalt not kill.

THOU SHALT NOT KILL.

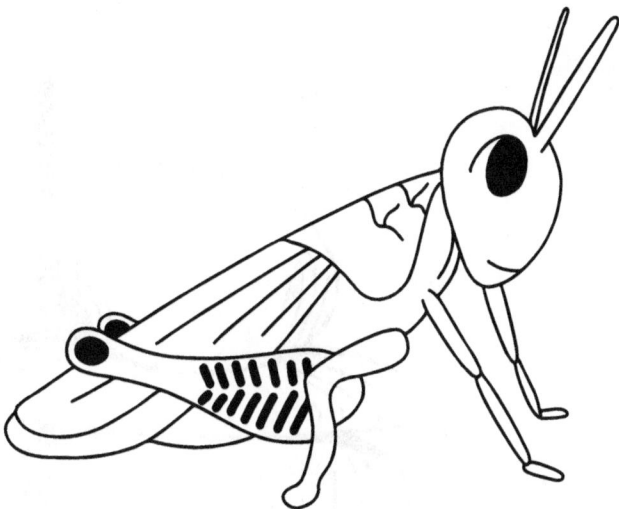

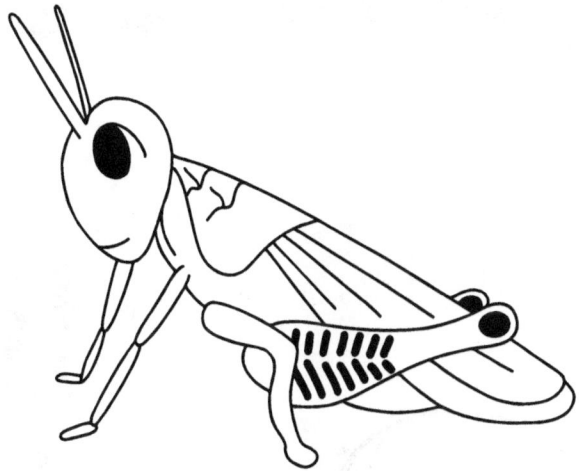

VII

Thou shalt not commit adultery.

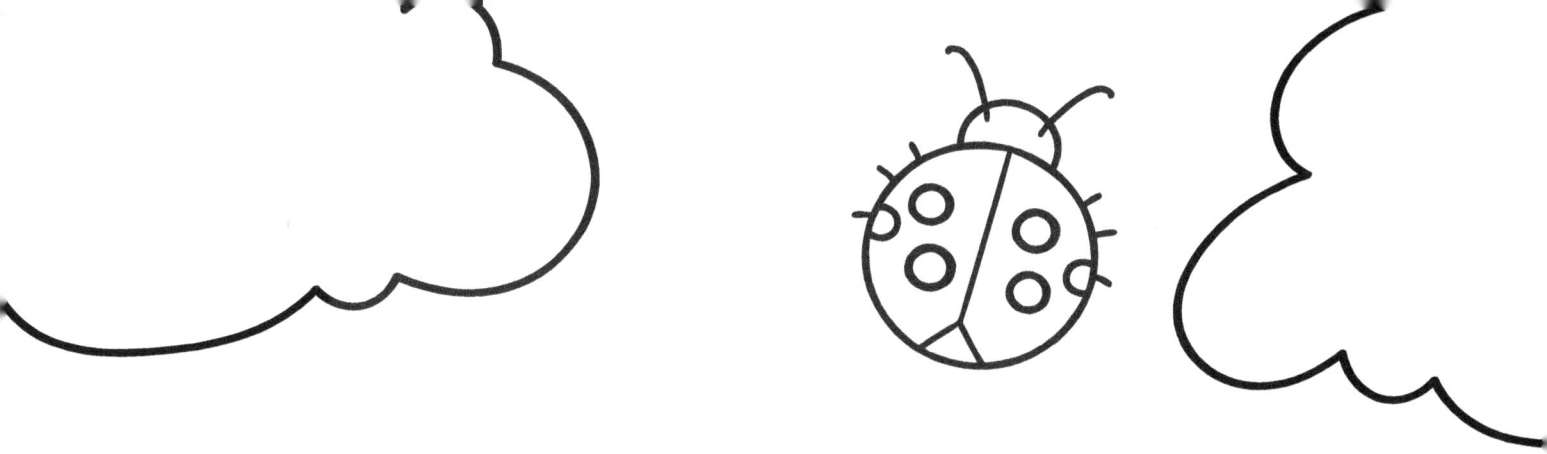

THOU SHALT NOT COMMIT ADULTERY.

VIII

Thou shalt not steal.

THOU SHALT NOT STEAL.

IX

Thou shall not bear false witness.

THOU SHALL NOT BEAR  FALSE WITNESS.

X

You shall not covet.

YOU SHALL NOT COVET.

EXODUS 20:20
AND MOSES SAID UNTO THE PEOPLE, FEAR NOT: FOR GOD IS COME TO PROVE YOU, AND THAT HIS FEAR MAY BE BEFORE YOUR FACES, THAT YE SIN NOT.

TEN

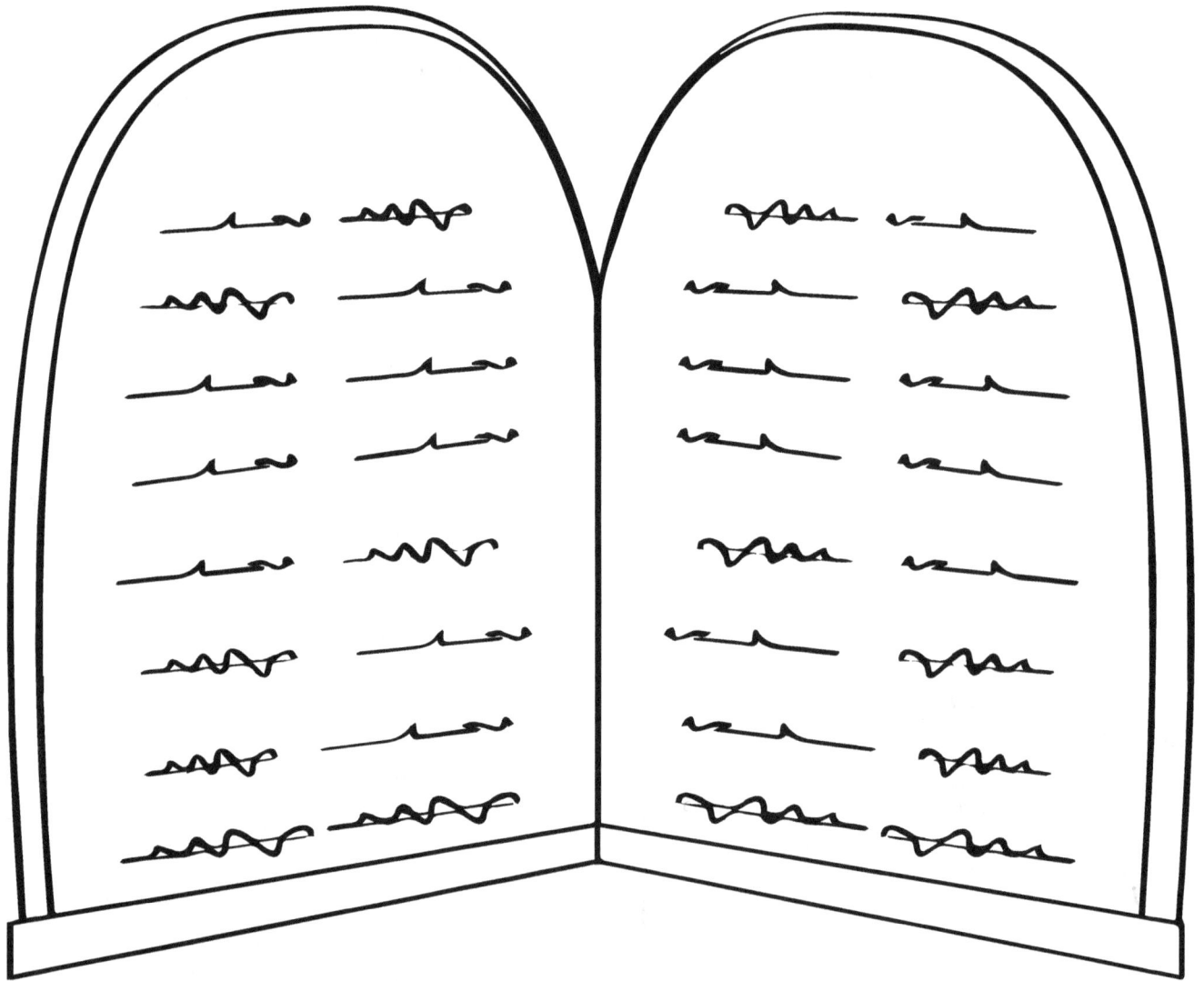

COMMANDMENTS

www.ingramcontent.com/pod-product-compliance
Lightning Source LLC
Chambersburg PA
CBHW080636040426
42331CB00048B/3182